Understanding Chinese Painting

T.C. Lai

With an Essay on Modern Chinese Painting:
Tradition and Innovations
by

Wucius Wong

SCHOCKEN BOOKS · NEW YORK

CONTENTS

First American edition published by Schocken Books 1985
10 9 8 7 6 5 4 3 2 1   85 86 87 88
Copyright © 1980 by T.C. Lai
All rights reserved
Published by agreement with The Swindon Book Company,
   Kowloon, Hong Kong

Library of Congress Cataloging in Publication Data
Lai, T.C.
   Understanding Chinese painting.
   Reprint. Originally published: Hong Kong: Kelly & Walsh, c1980.
   1. Painting, Chinese.   2. Painting, Chinese — Technique.
   3. Painting — Technique.   I. Title.
ND1040.L35   1985   759.951   84-23467

Printed in Hong Kong
ISBN 0-8052-3960-X

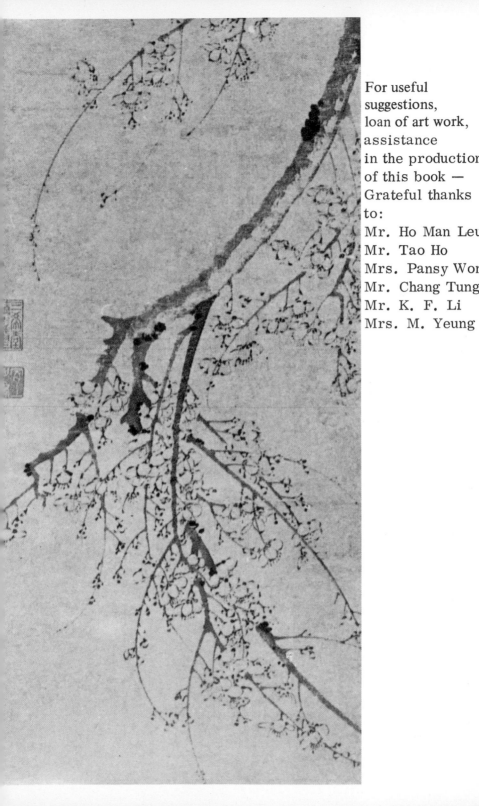

For useful
suggestions,
loan of art work,
assistance
in the production
of this book —
Grateful thanks
to:
Mr. Ho Man Leuk
Mr. Tao Ho
Mrs. Pansy Wong
Mr. Chang Tung
Mr. K. F. Li
Mrs. M. Yeung

論畫以形似見與兒童
鄰賦詩必此詩是知
非詩人詩畫本一律天
工與清新　東坡詩

FOREWORD

This book is my long-delayed tribute to Chinese painting — the most important aspect of Chinese art.

It is an attempt to make Chinese painting less baffling to the layman and help him acquire an attitude as well as some knowledge necessary to an enjoyment and understanding of the art. The emphasis is on how to appreciate Chinese paintings without having to be entangled in its history and aesthetic theories.

In the process of writing, my work has been greatly facilitated by the generous help given by Mr. Chuang Shen, Head of the Department of Fine Art, University of Hong Kong. I am grateful to him for allowing me to draw on his wide knowledge of Chinese painting and for supplying a number of illustrations for the chapter on Composition and Perspective.

In maintaining a uniform quality of the text, I am indebted to Mrs. Monica Lai, a Lecturer at the Department of English and Comparative Literature of the University of Hong Kong, for her valuable suggestions.

For giving an additional dimension to the project, I wish to thank Mr. Wucius Wong, a Principal Lecturer at the Hongkong Polytechnic for the essay on Tradition and Innovations in Modern Chinese Painting which provides provoking ideas on its future. It was written independently and without reference to the ideals and preferences implicit in the contents of this book.

T. C. L.

Chinese Painting Is Written

Chinese Painting Is Written

It would be too sweeping a statement to say that all Chinese painting is *written*.* But it is quite safe to say that the best Chinese paintings were done that way: at least the painters themselves would claim they *write* paintings. Pa Ta Shan Jan 八大山人 (1625–1705), in his earlier paintings usually signed *Pa Ta Shan Jan Hua* (*painted* by Pa Ta Shan Jan) but his later paintings usually bear the signature *Pa Ta Shan Jan Hsieh* (*written* by Pa Ta Shan Jan). The distinction was certainly meant to be taken seriously.

* Used in the sense of "writing a character or a piece of calligraphy" in which every stroke can be clearly accounted for.

One associates "writing a painting" with writing a character, a vague or not so vague image of which is already in the artist's mind before he puts pen to paper. The first stroke determines the configuration and movement of the character to be written, although as the writing proceeds the brush follows the impulses of the moment and makes necessary variations. It is similar in painting. The artist conceives an idea and sets out to substantiate his vision, his brush following his impulses and the dictates of the moment and *writes* it — very often employing the same kinds of brush strokes that he uses in calligraphy. In depicting a landscape, for instance, he does not attempt to copy the scene in reality before him, but captures what he sees and reconceives it in his own mind, then *writes* it so that the beholder of the result first enjoys it as a whole then starts to follow the movement of his brush and ruminates over the beauty of each stroke. Let us follow the way a painting is done by the late Ting Yin-yung*, acclaimed today as one of the most eminent artists who handle the brush in the traditional way.

It should be noted that Chinese painting is done on very absorbent paper, which demands complete control of the brush and ink so that the flow of ink and the way it spreads should be as the artist desires. No corrections or erasure can pass without injuring the painting. Every stroke can be accounted for and judged for merits or defects .

How a painting is *written* ▶

* T. C. Lai's THREE CONTEMPORARY CHINESE PAINTERS (University of Washington Press) contains an account of Ting Yin-yung and his art.

14

The start

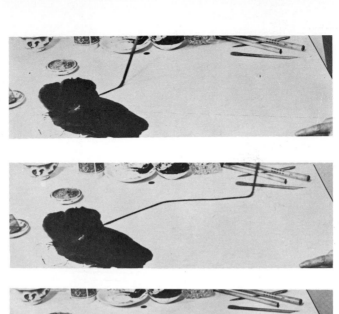

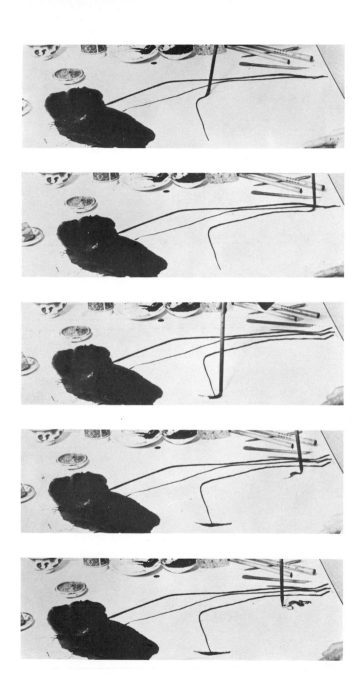

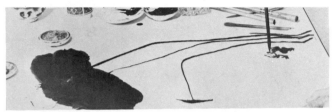

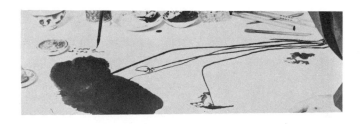

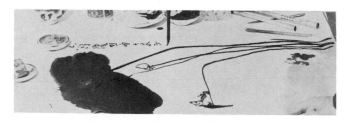

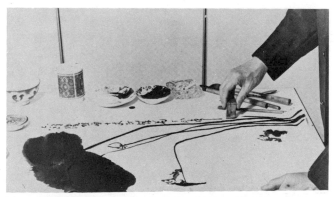

The artist putting his seal on the finished work, which is reproduced on p.20.

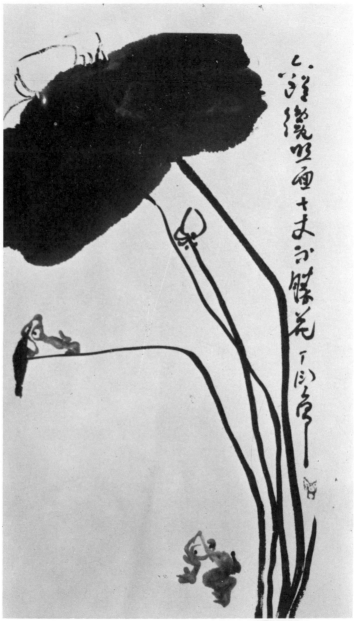

The finished painting: Lotuses and frogs.
The inscription:
The lotuses have just looked at themselves in the watery mirror;
The long stalks are slender and can hardly support the flowers.

The pictures on pages 22-26 are chosen for their clear-cut quality. Every stroke can be accounted for and enjoyed for its beauty, strength and verve. One can almost see the artist *writing* as if doing a piece of calligraphy.

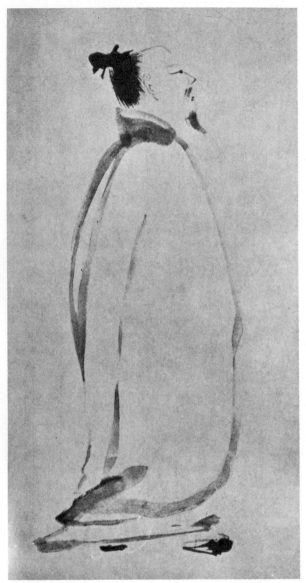

Li Po. L'iang Kai, fl. 1250.   Detail.

Portrait of a holy person. Kuan Tao Sheng.
The inscription: Painted in the manner of Wu Tao Tze in the fourth
month of the sixth year of Ta Teh 1306.   23

Landscape. Chang Feng, fl. 1640.

Birds. Pa Ta Shan Jen, 1625 - c. 1705.

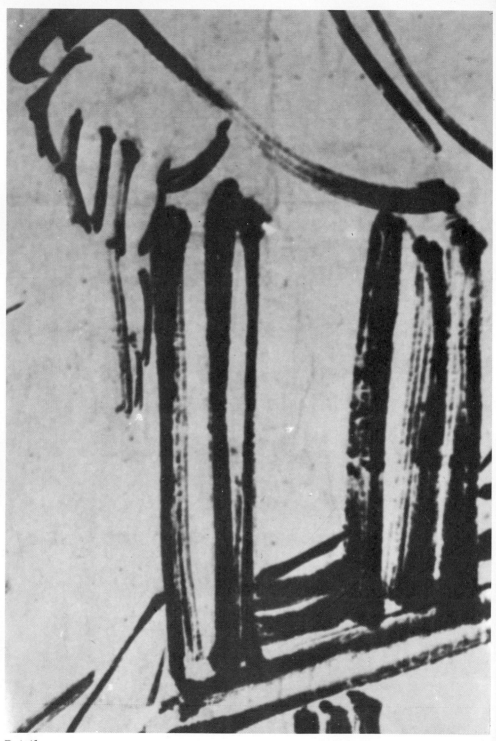

Detail.

Figures by Su Jen Shan, 19th C.

Opposite: Detail of a section of the picture above. The
enlarged strokes are about one-third of the actual size.
Note the calligraphic nature of the strokes.

Monk Sewing. Anon. The ink-on-paper painting, done in the manner of Mu Chi of the Sung Dynasty, is a fine example of graphic representation by clearly identifiable brush strokes.

The Brush Stroke

Before delving into the depths of the brush stroke, it is necessary to know something about the Chinese brush. Its tip consists of long, thin springy hairs effectively fitted together. Around a core consisting of the longest hairs is a layer of shorter hairs, which in turn are enveloped by several long hairs, creating a small hollow space between the core and the outer layer as a reservoir to hold the ink. When a good brush is lifted after pressure on the paper, it automatically resumes its original shape.

This Sung painting, attributed to Su Shih, is distinguished for the powerful strokes.

Thus the Chinese brush is preeminently a line instrument, which was probably first given its shape in answer to the demands of calligraphy.

A typical brush stroke may be a straight line, a dot, a curve, a hook, or a blot of any shape, characterised by a rhythmic alternation of thickness and thinness within each stroke or a multiplicity of them, giving the calligraphy or painting great charm.

The expressive possibilities of the brush are infinite. Every brush stroke is a force from the energy of the man who writes or draws it. The trained viewer and critic can read the vigour (strength) of the brush stroke, and its expression. From these he may also draw inferences regarding the writer's temperament and intellectual powers.

The aesthetics of the brush stroke is very difficult to describe. The viewer must either grasp it, or not at all, after considerable exposure to good calligraphy and painting. Nevertheless, it is necessary to bear in mind that during the first six centuries A.D. the calligraphic brush stroke was the dominant means of expression in Chinese painting, with the result that the theory of painting was closely based on that of calligraphy. In addition to its function of depicting objects, the individual brush stroke also possessed an independent value of its own as a means of expression. One can see the breath of life, as it were, in a single stroke.

Shih T'ao in his "Friar Bitter-Melon on Painting" said that an artist should be able to depict the universe in one stroke; that myriad of strokes in a painting must begin here and end here; that the stroke, if used skilfully, can be made to show all the complexities of nature and life.

The first brush stroke is the deciding step in a Chinese painting. The brush stroke may be made with light or heavy ink, with a wet or dry brush, with an even or varying pressure on the hand, with the brush held perpendicularly or at an angle — the character of the painting will be determined by it.

In other words, the brush stroke is the basic structural element of all painting. Swift or slow, delicate or heavy strokes — as the occasion demands — are valued for their own sake. When these are well done, they bear an imprint as personal as the artist's handwriting.

The characteristics of an artist's handwriting are repeated, even if in a modified form, in the brush strokes of his painting.

The individuality of a Chinese painter's handwriting as expressed in his painting is a matter of nuance, and necessitates a very careful study of brush strokes before one can recognise the individual touch of a master behind the styles and mannerisms that belong to his period in general.

Everything that the Chinese painter produces on his painting surface, in all its thousands of variations, derives originally from exactly the same principles as the simple brush stroke of calligraphy, although in painting the possibilities are far wider and richer.

The Chinese invented a method of thickening and thinning "brush" contours to suggest plasticity. "Brush" has always remained the chief means of representing forms.

"Brush" contour was used to convey the undulating movement of, for instance, drapery, instead of descriptive light as used by the West.

The artist, in depicting certain phenomena in reality, inevitably expresses his emotional response to these phenomena in the way he commands his brush; his emotion is inextricably involved in the activity of his brush, leaving traces in the strokes, be they short or long lines, dots or spots.

To know how to use a brush is not merely to know how to handle it in order to produce "force," but to know how to use the force to express certain emotional responses.

Thus disciplining the brush is a basic requirement in Chinese painting, a discipline which enables the artist to express emotion by the "force" of his brush stroke.

A line which expresses joy or peace of mind is usually one which runs fluently, goes unimpeded and shows no "corners" even in making a turn — no matter if the line is angular, round, slender, bold in shape, or dry, wet, dense or light.

Full appreciation of Chinese painting thus depends a great deal on the spectator's sensibility to the tempo and movement of the brush. He follows it as it dots, flicks, progresses, sweeps, turns, lifts, plunges, swells, poises to dart . . . .

That there is a very close relationship between painting and writing is well-established. From the very beginning the two arts served similar practical and intellectual ends.

Just as the writer must observe the fundamental form and structure of traditional signs or characters, the shape of which remain predetermined, so the painter must be able to handle freely the traditional pictorial signs or type forms which constitute his artistic vocabulary. These pictorial signs are the evidences of essential reality distilled through centuries of observation of transient effects. The mastery of type forms is essential to any artistic proficiency.

It was not until the seventeenth century that a comprehensive manual containing a synthesis of the traditional methods of study and aesthetic appreciation was published, complete with woodcut illustrations of the type forms used in painting in the past. This is the *Chieh tzu yüan hua chuan*, or Mustard Seed Garden Manual of Painting. This has since become an indispensable tool for art students. The type forms included therein are not only useful as convenient "alphabets" in painting, but also serve as expressive symbols for the artist's visions or associative ideas. It must be emphasized that he is less concerned with the faithful reproduction of transient phenomena than with the rendering of the typical features in them to serve as his expressive symbols. Through systematic training, he can use these type forms almost as freely as written characters, to "write" down his feelings in quick decisive strokes — and that cannot be done simply by representing the formal likeness.

Types of Brush Strokes
Selections from *Chieh Tzu Yüan Hua Chuan*

The Chieh Tzu Yuan Hua Chuan, or Mustard Seed Garden Manual of Painting, was published in Nanking by Shen Hsin-you, whose father-in-law was the famous writer Li Yu (1611-1680). The latter wrote the preface to the first edition, and people have since thought that he was the author. In fact, the brothers Wang Kai, Wang Nieh and Wang Shih were the creators.

The book contains descriptions and illustrations of type-forms in Chinese painting: type-forms of trees, rocks, figures, the orchid, the bamboo, the plum, the chrysanthemum, grasses, insects and flowering plants, and feathers-and-fur.

The manual became at one time the most widely used handbook of painting, and was acclaimed as a unique summary of the ideals and standards established by masters of Chinese painting.

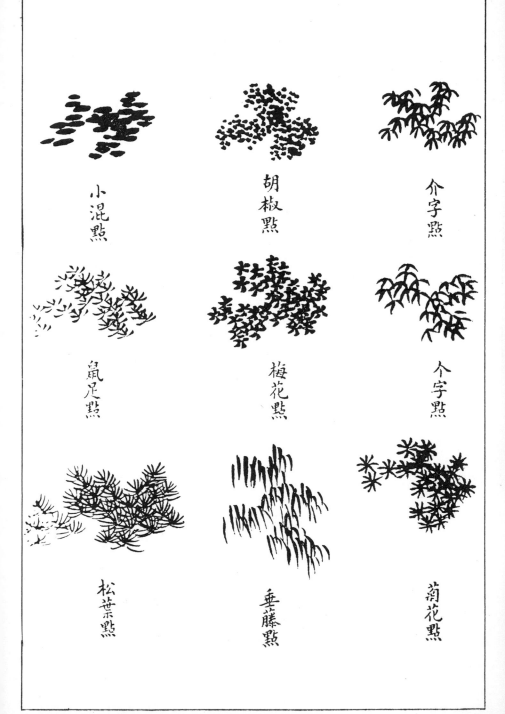

Brushstrokes (dotting) for various types of leaves.

此葉宜先着草綠然後填石綠

此葉填石青石綠俱可

此葉先着花青後填石青

此葉先着黃色草綠後填石綠膘

此葉着黃綠色或嫩黃色填綠襯綠俱可

此葉宜上三辮着脂濃綠下三辮着石綠或襯填石綠或用滕黃尖石綠上像婆羅樹栗

此葉宜着黃色或嫩黃者紅葉或硃或脂亦可

此葉或着青或綠或襯青綠俱可

此葉宜着赭色或紅葉

Leaves in outline.

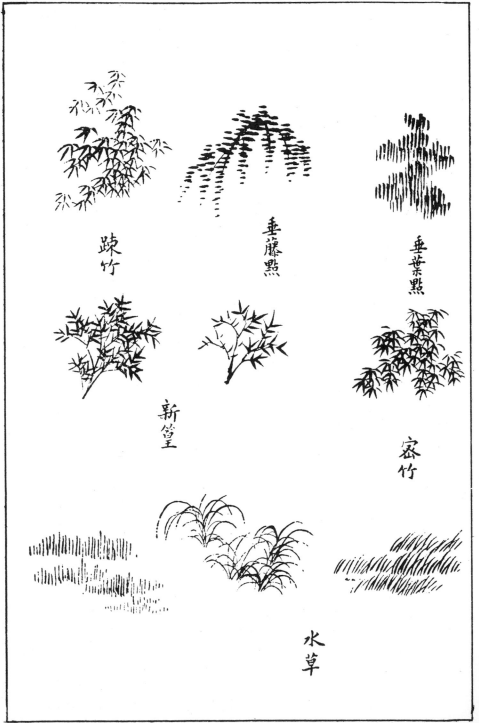

疎竹

垂藤點

垂葉點

新篁

密竹

水草

Brush strokes for bamboo leaves, hanging vine, water grass, etc.

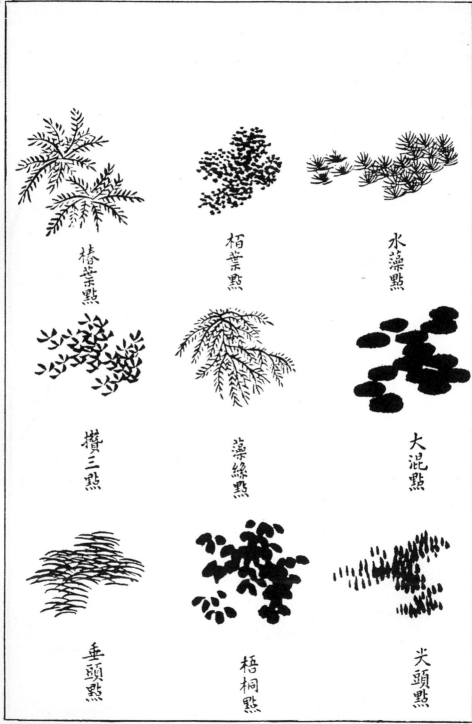

椿葉點　栢葉點　水藻點

攢三點　藻絲點　大混點

垂頭點　梧桐點　尖頭點

Brush strokes for leaves, grass, etc.

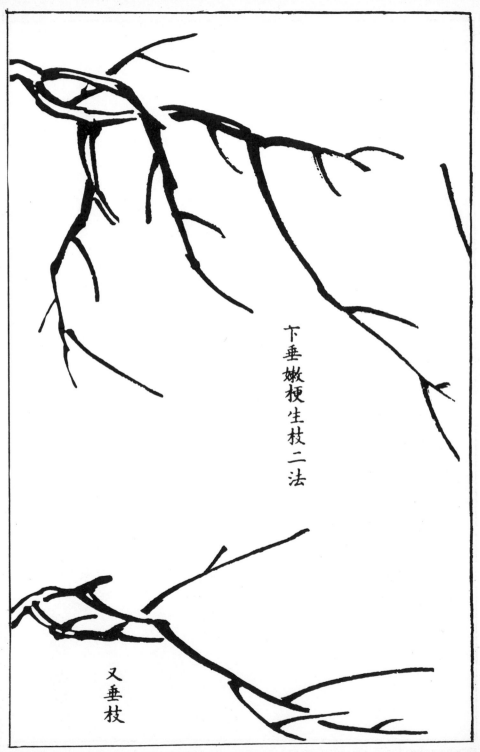

下垂嫩梗生枝二法

又垂枝

Twigs growing from hanging branches.

四筆落雁

Bamboo leaves.

雙竿生枝

Branches growing from two stems.

Two orchid plants with leaves crossing.

兩叢交互

凡畫兩叢須知有賓有主
有照有應於半空處著花
根邊小葉一名釘頭不可
太多熟極自能生巧

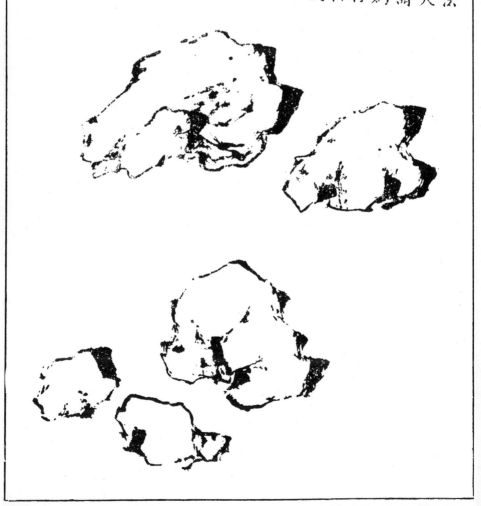

畫石起手當分三面法
觀人者必曰氣骨石乃天
地之骨而氣亦寓焉故謂
之曰雲根無氣之石則為
頑石猶無骨之石則為
骨堂有朽骨而可施於驕
人韻士筆下乎是無氣
之石固不可而畫有氣之
石即氣於無可提琴之
中尤難乎其難非胸中煉
有媧皇指上立有顛末未
可從事而我今以為無難
也蓋石有三面三面者即
石之凹深凸淺參合陰陽
步伍高下辨量厚薄以及
碧頭菱面員其胎泉此難
石之勢也熟此而氣亦隨
勢以生矣秘法無多請以
三金針相告口活

Rocks.

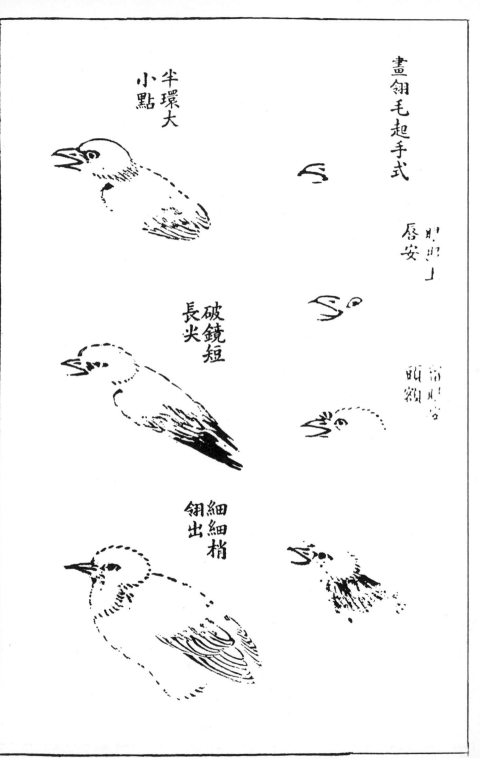

First steps in painting birds.

徐徐小
尾填

羽毛翅
脊後

脳肚腿
肶前

展

臨了繞
添脚

拳

Continued from last page.

山水中鳥獸各式此種雖
屬細事然所關者甚大如
要畫春春畫不出第畫一
鳴鳩乳燕非春而何如要
畫秋秋畫不出第畫一飛
鴻宿雁非秋而何然此猶
於山樹可以分別者也至
要畫曉曉畫不出第畫棲
鳥出林吠厐守戶非曉而
何要畫暮暮畫不出第畫

雙馬飲泉式

負驢式

Horses and donkeys.

釣魚式

吹簫式

撥阮式

鳴絃吹笛式

燒丹式

漁家聚飲式

獨坐看花式

Figure drawing.

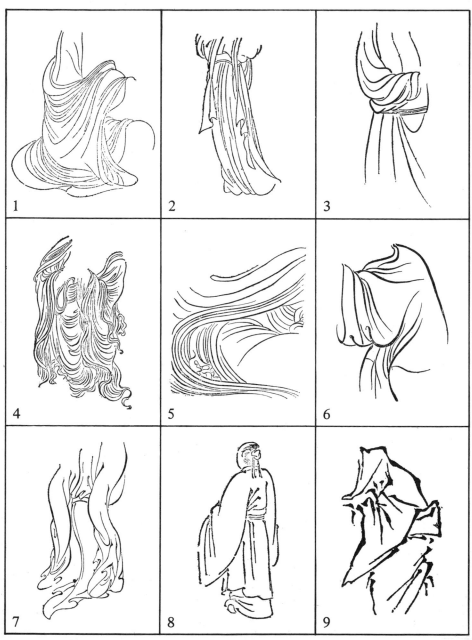

18 types of strokes (from 金原省吾著線の研究):
1. Gossamer strokes   2. Zither string strokes   3. Steel wire strokes
4. Flying clouds and Flowing water strokes   5. Ts'ao Garment strokes
6. Earth worm strokes   7. Orchid-leaf strokes   8. Nail-head rat-tail
strokes   9. Upright nail-head strokes

10. Willow-leaf strokes   11. Bamboo-leaf strokes   12. Mixed strokes
13. Broken reed strokes   14. Date-stone strokes   15. Olive strokes
16. Undulating ripple strokes   17. Dried wood strokes   18. Abbreviated strokes

"Force"

Having achieved proficiency in the language of the type forms in painting, the artist must then endow each brush stroke he makes with refinement. This consists in what is called "force," an abstraction the constituents of which are "muscle, flesh, bone and spirit."* The connoisseur first views a painting as a whole and then immediately proceeds to examine each part and scrutinise the strokes for virtuosity and maturity. He enjoys good strokes in a painting as he would in calligraphy.

The paintings on pages 54 — 68 are selected for the "force" and refinement exhibited in some of the brush strokes.

*See page 233 under Four Types of Force in Brushwork.

The painting of Fu Shan (opposite page) seems to have been "written" entirely with calligraphic brush strokes, especially when viewed together with his calligraphy on this page, done in seal script.

This figure by Ch'iu Ying is a good example of delicately executed lines used to convey undulating movements of drapery.

This picture of a Lohan and his tiger by Shih K'o demonstrates how a skilful artist can use a broken brush to great advantage.

Landscape. Hsu Wei (1521-1593). The apparently haphazard way in which the over-hanging cliff was executed belies the extraordinary virtuosity of the painter.
The inscription was addressed to Hsu's teacher who, according to the poem, had to take up an appointment, against his own inclination, in order to support his young children.

流水開花此不雲
葛月心作山

This painting by Chen Sui (1605–1691) is distinguished for the skilful use of the dry-brush strokes, all of which can be accounted for and enjoyed.

◀ This painting by Fu Shan (1602–1683) impresses with the skilful use of apparently disjointed lines formed by a combination of strokes in which much of the beauty of the picture lies.

Detail of a painting by Shih T'ao. The lines, accentuated by light dots, are full
of power and nervous energy.

This painting of rocks and daffodils by Huang Shen clearly demonstrates to what extent brush strokes in painting and calligraphy can be related.

昌蒲九節俯潭清飲水仙人綠骨輕踏草林花空識面肯從塵土論交情

文田先生良友有道之教

七十二翁杭郡金農畫詩書

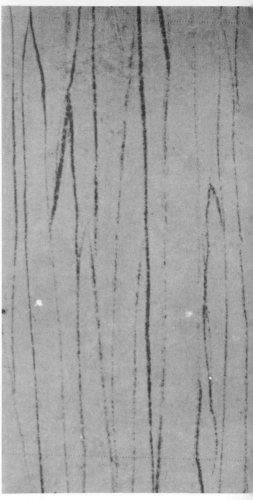

Detail.

Calami. Chin Nung, 1687 - 1764.

The inscription:
The nine-joint calami lean over a clear
    pond;
Green-boned immortals, here they
    take their drink.
The lowly grass and flowers know
    them by sight —
Would these tall reeds stoop to be
    their friends?

The Calamus, or Sweet Flag (Ch'ang-p'u), a medi-
cinal plant thought to be an elixir in Taoist tradition.

Gourd and Vines: Ch'i Pai Shih. Interesting contrast between lines and ink wash and between light and dark surfaces. The inscription: Descendant of family who lived in Sheng T'ang Old House.

This picture of a monk meditating before an incense burner by Pu Hsin-yü, 1896-1963, is distinguished for the extraordinary simplicity and terseness of the brush strokes. The inscription: My heart is filled with yearning for Nirvana.

This painting of bamboos by Ch'i Pai Shih
shows how like calligraphic strokes the
leaves look, and how they harmonise with
the inscription.

"Cat" done with one stroke of the brush by Ting Yin-yung, 1903-1978.

Inscription on Chinese Painting

Inscription on Chinese Painting

A Chinese art enthusiast does not merely look at a painting. He reads it. He "reads" the shape, texture and individual strokes with their calligraphic nuances as well as what may be written on it. This chapter is mainly concerned with the latter — the inscriptions which form part of the paintings and constitute their artistic essence.

The total experience of looking at a Chinese painting therefore consists of enjoyment of the pictures and meditation on the poems and inscriptions — without which Chinese painting would be much poorer.

The first inscriptions on paintings were done in the time of the Warring States Period, 403-221 B.C., and popularised in the Han Dynasty, 206 B.C. to 219 A.D., when four-character compositions were written on portraits in praise of the persons concerned. The earliest inscription to record the origin of or to point a moral in a painting were probably done by Ku Kai Chih (345-411 A.D.) of the Ts'in Dynasty. Lu Hung, who flourished around 700 A.D., provided the first poetic inscription extant. Tu Fu (712-770 A.D.) and the literati artists of his time provided some inscriptions of this type, as can be seen from the poetry anthologies of this period. Poetic inscriptions reached the status of a literary genre in the Sung Dynasty when Su Shih (1036-1101 A.D.) and Huang T'ing Chien (1050-1100 A.D.) advanced the idea that poetic inspiration derives from the same source as pictorial inspiration. Poetry and painting were spoken of as on the same level of excellence. Thus Su Shih wrote:

To say that a painting should look like real life
Is to babble like ignorant children;
To want to create poetry but insist on the written form
Is to confess a non-poetic disposition.
Poetry and painting are one and the same thing:
The product of natural gift and freshness of vision.

His comment on the art of Wang Wei is well-known:

Examining a poem by Wang Wei,
one discovers its pictorial quality;
Meditating on a painting by Wang Wei,

one discovers its poetical essence.

That gave rise to the popular aphorism that poetry is verbal painting and painting is non-verbal poetry.

Thereafter, poetic inscriptions became so popular that anthologies on them were published as early as the 12th century. In the Ming Dynasty poetic inscriptions were the order of the day. By the Ching Dynasty some inscriptions not only occupied large parts of paintings, but they were also so placed and written as to be aesthetically bound up with the total visual experience of the works themselves.

The main function of an inscription is to shed light on the artist's purpose or basic idea: to help the onlooker see more clearly the artist's intentions.

An inscription may be descriptive; it may tell a story; it may be concerned with the technique of painting — the composition, the particular style adopted by the artist or some discussion on artistic theory. Inscriptions are normally written by the painters themselves; but often they are written by others, who may include friends of the painter, fellow artists, collectors or connoisseurs. They may contain criticism or approbation from another painter, an eminent scholar or politician, or even the sovereign himself.

The brushwork used in a painter's own inscription usually harmonizes with the painting, a harmony not merely of line, but of mood. Thus inscriptions can be important guides to the collector for testing the genuineness of a work of art. In fact the painter's own inscription is often the determining factor. The truth is it is easier to fake painting than to fake calligraphy.

▶

The picture is part of a long scroll commonly called "Admonitions of the Court Instructress" by Ku Kai Chih (c. 345-411).

It needs the following inscription to bring out its meaning: People all know how to beautify their persons but few know how to refine their personality by cultivating virtue; when this is neglected, a person may transgress against propriety and deviate from the correct path. So strive to correct and discipline yourself and conquer your passions in order to preserve virtue.

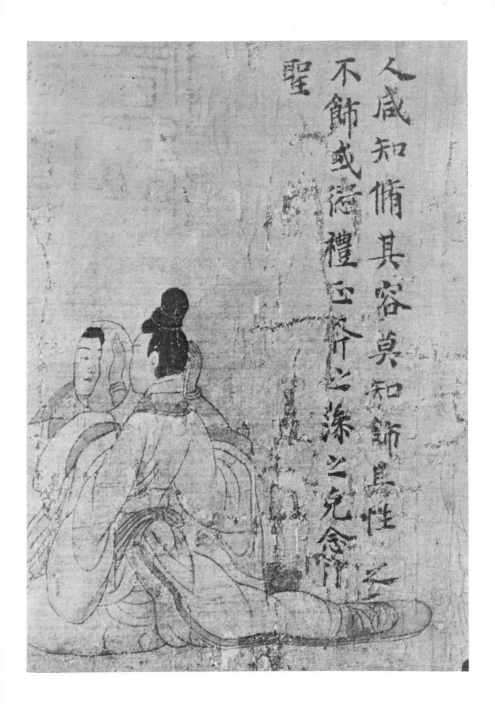

人咸知脩其容莫知飾其性之
不飾或愆德禮正於介之漸蘭兄念衿
聖

Pheasant. Emperor Hui Tsung of Sung.
The inscription:
The hibiscus is still flourishing despite autumn's
rigours.
On its bough stands a crested many-hued phea-
sant.
It has five virtues — beauty, strength, valour,
kindness, trust.
In its serenity it surpasses the wild duck and the
widgeon.

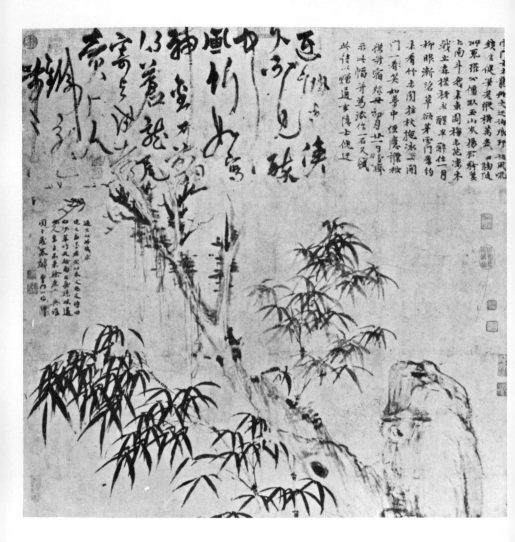

Old Tree, Bamboo and Rock. A joint effort by Ni
Tsan, Ku An and Chang Shen. (Yuan Dynasty)
Part of the inscription says: Hsueh Chai showed
me this picture and I added a rock to it together
with this poem. Ni Tsan.

This picture of quails by Pa Ta Shan Jen bears an inscription the meaning of which is quite obscure, perhaps intentionally so. It reads:

Had somehow a full day's chat;
One seems to be male, the other female;
Yellow gold and white sun
Do not come up to the expectations of Wu Fan
　　Erh.

The Yellow Mountains. Shih T'ao, 1641 - 1717.
The inscription:
   A few generous splashes from the inkstone,
   And lo! The wet cloud-patches
   Of the Yellow Mountain!
   Wong Wei is a great painter no doubt
   But who can distinguish his
   From this?
   Such spareness,
   Such rareness.

I suddenly recalled the thirty six peaks and
and wrote this. Monk Bitter Melon.

沅湖一段雲
花雨瀠濕黃
山幾段雲縱
是王維稱畫
手清奇難向
筆頭分
清湘苦瓜稱
尚忿憶三十六
峰寫此

乾隆元年應舉至
都門與徐亮直翰林過張司寇
忠司寇出觀趙王孫墨梅小立軸
冷香清艷展視摹人大倡予繼
塵浣素本也予一老僕人予布衾予緼
追寫寒葩不覺黯然自失恨不予二
老見我橫枝滿幅含豪作簡齋
詩句一題其上也
七十五叟農畫記

Plum Blossoms. Chin Nung, 1687 - 1764.
The inscription: In the first year of Ch'ien Lung, I
went to take the provincial examination in Tu
Mien, and with Hsa Chi-lang, a Hanlin, visited
Chang at his house. Chang entertained us by show-
ing a hanging scroll of plum blossoms by Chao.
The beholder is greeted by a cool and fragrant
breeze. It is thought-provoking. It reminds one
of "Dark dust over white robe." Now both Hsu
and Chang are gone and I myself am a declining
old man. When I try to paint the cool blossoms,
I feel a sense of great loss. I regret my friends
cannot be here to see the branches sprawling over
the paper and to inscribe some lines of poetry to
emulate that of Chen Chien Tsai. Old Man Chin
Nung at 75.

Detail

Artist Writing on a Wall. Chang Feng, fl. 1640. ▶
The inscription:
  Of the great calligraphers of Shan Yin, Wang was
    the greatest.
  The children, I am afraid, are ignorant of this.
  A Wang-addict, I am prone to being wine-rapt;
  Walking up, I would try my hand a little.

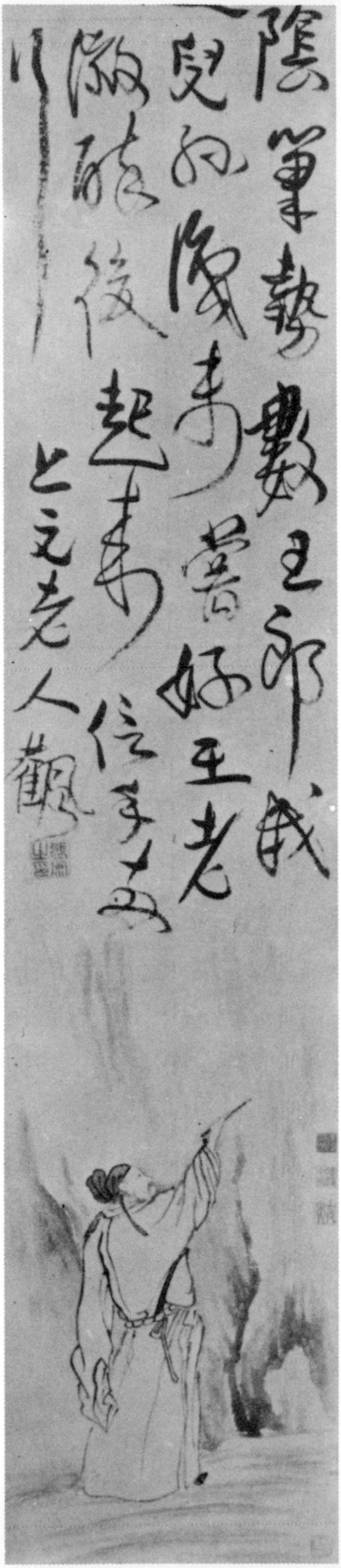

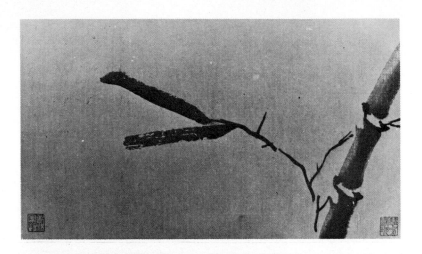

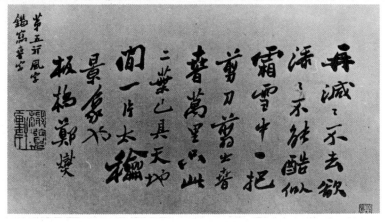

Bamboo. Li Fang Ying, 1695 - 1754.
The composition is simplicity itself. The artist's message is left to his friend Cheng Hsieh (1693 - 1765) to interpret. Cheng's inscription reads: Nothing. can be taken away; nothing can be added; they are like a pair of scissors which cuts its way through snow and frost to bring us ten thousand miles of spring breeze. These two leaves alone will call forth the image of a whole world of autumn's desolation.

三間茅閣草屋五里十里
松聲如此山中景色何時共
余同作二樵人韵篁
〔印〕

Sylvan Joy. Li Chien
1747 - 1799.

The inscription:
Two or three thatched
    cottages;
Five or ten miles of
    pine-song;
With such sound and
    beauty in the
    mountains —
When are you going to
    take a stroll with
    me?

Bamboo Fence. Lo P'in, 1733 - 1809.

The inscription:

I had painted a fence of plum trees when my servant-boy came to tell me this: A monk of the Golden Grain Temple had bent a row of bamboos into a fence. They must be suffering a great deal from the bondage. Why don't you paint the agony of these tall, slender gentlemen?

So I did this for fun. Lo P'in the twin-peak scholar.

Composition and Perspective

Composition and Perspective

Since the 5th century, landscape painting in China has always been called by the term *Shan-Shui*, literally meaning "mountain and water." Although the term has much wider implications, to include, for instance, hills, valleys, cliffs, rivers, rapids, brooks, waterfalls, lakes, etc., a Chinese landscape painting appears to the casual viewer to be little more than a design which emphasizes balance between mountain and stream, between mass and void, or between solidity and fluidity.

One of the characteristics of a Chinese landscape painting (and for that matter, other types of painting) is the way the artist represents distance, height and depth. This was systematized in the 10th century into three main types of composition, according to the ways the three dimensions are related and contrasted.

(1) *High-distance Composition.* The type of composition in which a mountain is seen from below is called "high-distance" or "high perspective." The earliest example of this type is Fan Kan's "Travellers among Mountains and Streams." (P. 95)

Another example is the well-known "Early Spring" dated 1072 by Kuo Hsi, with a somewhat more complicated composition. (P. 96)

High–distance composition

(2) *Flat-distance Composition.* Another type of composition in which the viewer looks toward the distance is called "flat distance" or "level perspective." The "Wintry Forest and Multi-shores" by Tung Yüan from the late 10th century seems to be the earliest example of this category. In this picture, the representation of depth is successfully done by three sections of triangular shores, one in front of another. (P. 99)

Ni Tsan's small hanging scroll entitled "The Jüng-Chi Studio" dated 1372 successfully gives a flat-distance impression. (P. 100)

The picture by Wang Yüan-chi (1642-1715) is obviously modelled upon Ni Tsan's. (P. 101)

The painting by Su Jen-shan (mid-19th century) is a variation of this type. (P. 102)

Flat–distance composition

(3) *Deep-distance Composition.* The landscape is seen, as it were, as a bird's eye view. Sizes of things do not appear to vary in spite of the distances apart. The 17th century's copy of a "snow scene" attributed to Li Cheng (10th century) serves as the earliest example of this type. Two compositions which represent upward movement — though not designed to give an indication of height but rather to give an impression of depth — are "Buddhist Temple Among Snowy Mountains" by Ch'ien Ku (1508-1572) and "Snowscape" by Chang Ku. (PP. 105 and 106)

Deep-distance composition

Travellers among mountains and streams.
Fan Kan, late 10th century.

樹纔發葉溪
湖凍綠初仙
居家上層不
藉梅開致
似春山早兄
氣如茶
乙卯春月
溈老

Early Spring. Kuo Hsi, dated 1072.

96

Landscape. Li Tsai, 15th century.

Landscape attributed to Shubun, 15th century. A Japanese conception of "high distance."

Wintry Forest and Multi-shores. Tung Yuan, late 10th century.

The Yung Chi Studio. Ni Tsan, dated 1372.

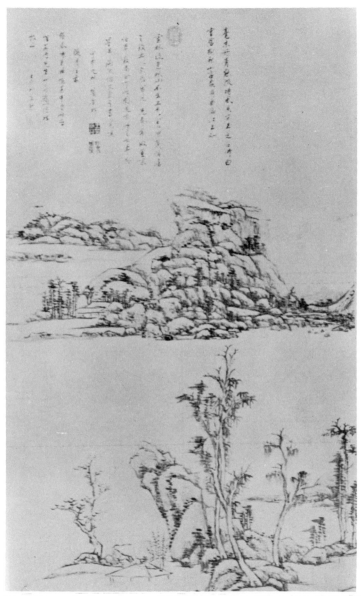

Landscape, in the manner of Ni Tsan. Wang Yüan-chi, 1642-1715.

Landscape. Su Jen Shan, mid-19th century.

Snow Scene. 17th century copy of a painting attributed to
Li Cheng 10th century.

Landscape. Chang Ting, contemporary.

Snowy Mountains. Ch'ien Ku, dated 1564.

Mountain Path in Snow. Chang Ku, 17th C.

Music and Repast. Anon. Five Dynasties. Note the shape of the
long table.

A palatial complex in Yüan Ming Yüan. T'ang Tai and Shen Yüan.

Hsuan Wen Chün lecturing to scholars. Ch'en Hung-shou. Note ▶
various "levels" of perspective.

Ode of Pin. Anon (13th C.). Section of a long scroll (note the highly exaggerated size of the crickets under the couch).

Part of a scroll illustrating the Ode to the Red Cliff (II) by Su Shih.
Chiao Chung Ch'ang (12th century).

The Tai-ming Terrace. Section of a long scroll. Anon. (14th C.)

Symbolism in Chinese Painting

Symbolism in Chinese Painting

It is easy to forget the symbolic meaning of a Chinese painting when our attention is centered only upon its subject-matter, composition and technique. But often it is the symbolic aspect that dominates the theme of a painting — hence the necessity to discuss some of the natural objects that are associated with it.

The Pine Tree

A Chinese painting can be a pictorial representation of Chinese history and literature. Confucius (5th century B.C.) said: "In the cold season we realize that the pine and the cypress are the last to shed their leaves." The pine and the cypress are therefore looked upon as symbolic of the spirit of unyielding resistance and loftiness. The painting depicting a scholar seated beside a brazier in a cottage surrounded by tall pine trees is by Li Shan of the 17th century. (P. 117)

The poet T'ao Ch'ien (372-427), who chose to be a recluse rather than an official, was well-known for his love of pines and chrysanthemums. In his poem "Homeward Bound," he said: "In the fading twilight before darkness descends, I love to lean on a lonesome pine tree and linger awhile." The 16th century painting on page 118 succeeds in imparting a sense of loftiness and isolation.

Since the Sung Dynasty, the pine has also been associated with longevity. Kuo Hsi's son Kuo Sze edited "The Message of Forests and Streams," which contains a description of a painting by the former as follows: On a small piece of skill which measures a little more than two feet, my father painted an old man, under an exuberant pine tree, which leans on another one issuing from the side of a cliff. From here proceed innumerable interlocking pines all the way down to the brook. There must be more than a hundred pines which run on interminably. My father has never designed anything like this before. This particular picture was done as a birthday present for Wen Yen-po

Li Shan, 17th century.

A recluse and a lonesome pine. Anon. 16th century.

(1006-1097). The picture symbolizes a continuous succession of sons and grandsons of the Wen family. Wen Yen-po was greatly pleased by the painting.

Thus, it is clear that ever since the 11th century the pine has been used to symbolize longevity and prosperity.

Plum-Blossoms

Like the pine and the cypress, the plum-blossom
is the only flower that can withstand frosty weath-
er. Thus, it seems natural for the Chinese intellectual to use the plum-blossom also as a symbol of
endurance and fortitude. From the 11th century
onward, the plum-blossom has also acquired an
additional significance. Lin Pu (967-1028), a well-
respected hermit who lived on a hill overlooking
the West Lake of Hangchow, called plum-blossoms
his wife. Plum-blossoms have always served as a
popular subject in Chinese painting.

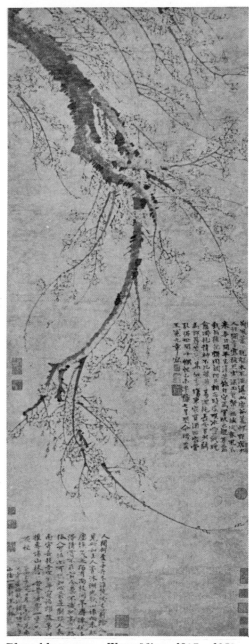

Plum-blossoms. Wang Mien, 1287 – 1358.

Bamboo

The bamboo is a very common plant in China. In the "Book of Songs," edited by Confucius, there are many references to bamboos. However, the bamboo was not given any symbolic value until the 4th century. In the early Eastern Chin period, Shan T'ao, Juan Chi, Liu Ling, Hsiang Hsiu, Chi Kang, Wang Jung and Juan Hsien were called "The Seven Sages of the Bamboo Grove." Similarly, in the T'ang period, the great poet Li Po lived together with five other literary men as recluses among bamboos and were called the "Six recluses among Bamboos near a brook." Wang Hsien-chih, a son of Wang Hsi-chih was also a well-known recluse scholar. He once said that he could not live without bamboos for a single day.

Bamboo. Ko Chiu Szu, 1312 - 1365.

Chrysanthemums. Wu Kung Tsai, Ching Dynasty.

Chrysanthemum

Until the 4th century, the chrysanthemum was regarded as a life-prolonging herb effective against rheumatism. However, since its close association with T'ao Ch'ien, it has become a symbol of the life of a recluse.

The chrysanthemum is often grouped together with the orchid, the bamboo and the plum-blossom to form what is now commonly called "The Four Gentlemen."

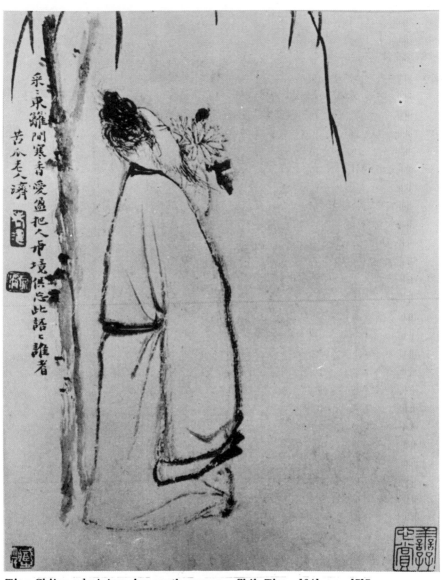

采东篱间寒香爱盈把人弄境供忘此语谁者

苦瓜老人濟

T'ao Ch'ien admiring chrysanthemums.   Shih T'ao, 1641 - c. 1717.
The inscription: Bright amidst the eastern hedges,
                  How I love their cold fragrance,
                  Here I forget myself and where I am;
                  How can I explain this to others.

The Five Pure Things

The Five Pure Things consist of the bamboo, the plum blossom, the pine, the moon and flowing water.

Five Pure Things. Yun Shuo Ping, Ching Dynasty.

127

Cranes. Attr. Huang Chuan, Five Dynasties
Period.

The Crane

The crane is a symbol of longevity and is often
seen carrying on its back the philosopher Lao Tze.
It is often associated with the recluse. The poet Lin
Pu of the Sung Dynasty, in his retirement, called
cranes his sons and plum-blossoms his wives.

Crane. Mu Chi, Sung Dynasty.

The Three Friends of Winter

Since the 13th century, the pine, the bamboo and the plum-blossom have been collectively called the "Three Friends of Winter."

The album leaf by Chao Meng-chien (1199-1295), depicting the pine, plum-blossoms and bamboo looks like a formal design. This innocent-looking picture however has a poignant hidden meaning. It represents the feelings of the Sung loyalists against the Mongol invaders. The incorruptibility of the pine, the uprightness of the bamboo and the purity of heart of the plum-blossoms are qualities which were incompatible with any sympathy with the new regime.

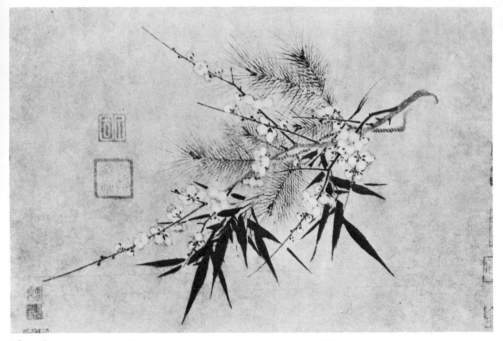

The Three Friends of Winter.   Chao Meng-chien, 1199-1295.

The Peach

The peach is a symbol of immortality, deriving from the myth that the God of Long Life was born from a peach. The Monkey in *The Journey to the West* stole the peaches of immortality from the heavenly reign and was punished with being chained and imprisoned underneath a rock. The inscription on the picture by Wu Chang-shih reads as follows:

The thousand-year old peaches are large as ladles.
They are picked by the immortals for making wine.
Those who eat them will have very long life
And always look like a youth of eighteen or nineteen.

Peaches. Wu Chang Shih, 1844 - 1927.

A Lotus Blossom. Anon. Sung Dynasty.

The Lotus

The lotus is a symbol of purity because it emerges
from muddy waters without being defiled. It is the
emblem of Ho Hsien Ku, one of the eight Taoist
immortals, who is depicted as holding a lotus-pod
cup. It is also associated with the Buddhist faith.

Lotuses. Li Chan, Ching Dynasty.

Mandarin Ducks

Mandarin ducks are usually associated with conjugal bliss and they are always shown in pairs.

Mandarin Ducks. Anon. Sung Dynasty.

The Carp

The carp is associated with success in examination. Traditionally success in examination means success in life. In Chinese mythology, the carp gets past the rapids of Dragon Gate and changes into a dragon. The symbolic meaning is that once a scholar passes the Imperial Examination, he becomes a success in the mandarinate.

The Carp. Ch'i Pai-shih, 1863-1957.
The inscription:
This painting by me was done at the
age of twenty. I am now over ninety
and see it again for the first time.
There is a lapse of some seventy
years. Naturally, there are differences in the brush-and-ink work and
I cannot help sighing when I record
this. Pai Shih at 91, still in Peking.

The Gourd

The gourd is a symbol of mystery. It is the universe in a nutshell. The Chinese phrase "What is in your gourd?" means "What are you hiding?" It is the emblem of Iron Crutch Li, one of the Eight Immortals. The inscription on the picture opposite says: "Every year the same things happen," alluding to the idiom "drawing according to the model of a gourd." It really means "Nothing exciting happens; everything remains the same."

The Wild Duck

The wild duch or *yen* is a migratory bird. It symbolises the carrier of messages from distant lands. Thus the Chinese phrase "to communicate by wild ducks or fish" means to correspond by letter.

The Ling Chih

The *ling chih* is a fungus with purplish stalk which will keep for a long time and is reputed to be a cure-all. It symbolizes long life and prosperity and is often the object of search by recluses.

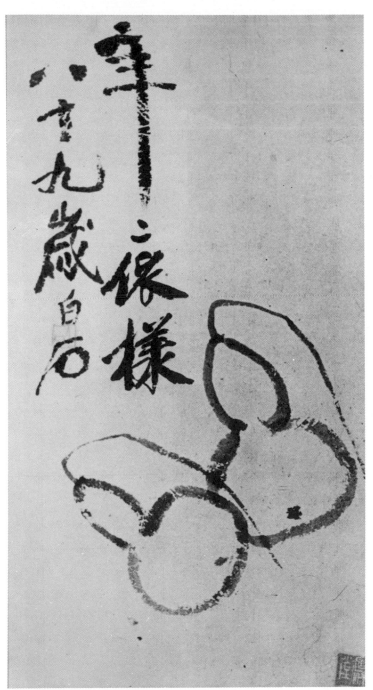

Gourds. Ch'i Pai-shih.

An immortal carrying a gourd. Shen Chou, 1472-1509.

Wild Ducks. Pien Shuo-min, active 1725-1747.

Ling Chih fungus and plum-blossoms. Fu Chi, 19th C.

The Broom

The broom is a symbol of insight and wisdom: it sweeps away all everyday cares and anxieties. It is associated with the poet-monk Shih-te of the T'ang Dynasty.

Monk with Broom. Chin Nung, 1687 - 1764. ▶
The inscription reads: Sprinkling water and sweeping the floor are the first duties of a Buddhist disciple.
The young and old monks alike should all work hard at this . . .

佛門以灑掃為第一執事自沙彌至老禿無不
早起勤作也香林有塔掃而洗洗而又掃舍利放
大光明不在塔中而在手中矣
蘇伐羅吉薩伐羅記

Paintings for Appreciation

Roasting.   Part of a wall painting.   First century B. C.   Excavated in Loyang, Hona

Painting on paper. Tsin Dynasty (4th - 5th C.).
Unearthed in Sinkiang in 1964. Juvenile — nevertheless done with a brush.

It is interesting to compare this with the painting
by Ku Kai Chih of the same period (page 75).

Mountains in Snow, attributed to Wang Wei (699-759) the T'ang Dynasty poet-painter. The Sung poet Su Shih said of Wang Wei: "There is painting in his poetry, and poetry in his painting." The scene probably represents a part of the environs in which Wang Wei took up residence in his latter days.

Before the T'ang Dynasty, landscape was used only as an accessary to figure painting, a secondary role which soon developed into an independent one. Wang Wei was one of the first to use only water and ink to paint landscape and is considered the founder of the Southern school of painting.

The Old Scholar by Wang Wei, T'ang Dynasty. This picture is often referred to as possessing "rhythmic vitality."

The T'ang Dynasty picture painted on wood has a child-like quality, almost abstract in the manner the lines are done. It has an antique flavour.

155

Bamboo. Wen Tung, 11th century.
This apparently simple composition is done with consummate skill worthy of one of the great painters of the bamboo. The calligraphic strokes are most skilfully structured, and one perceives extraordinary subtle use of ink tones. The leaves are probably done in the *Chung Feng* brush technique, in which the artist holds the brush in an upright position throughout the length of the stroke. In spite of the great number of leaves, there is uncompromising orderliness. One does not tire of looking at it although the subject matter seems so bare of content.

Bamboo. Wen Tung.

A typical Sung landscape characterised by skilful use of ink wash rather than line. The clouds are ball-shaped and present a three-dimensional illusion. Adoration of nature is the theme — nature garbed in an ever-changing sea of clouds.

Cranes that bring good fortune. Emperor Hui
Tsung of Sung. A colophon is attached to this
scroll of cranes, also by Emperor Hui Tsung, which
reads (abridged):

One evening in the 2nd year of Cheng Ho (1112
A.D.) clouds of varied colours were seen hovering
above the palace gates. Suddenly a flock of white

cranes came dancing, to the great surprise and joy of all who saw them. They stayed for quite a while before leaving. I believed they were harbingers of good fortune. How graceful they are, how fit to be companions of the Immortals in the isle of Peng Lai! I wrote a poem to commemorate the event.

Detail.

Spring in a Mountain Forest. Wang Meng (d. 1385).

The composition is compact. The hills (the backbone of the composition) and trees fill the whole surface from top to bottom, thus appearing rather overcrowded at first sight. The main elements of the design are deeply folded and creviced rocks rising precipitously. The undulating "wrinkles" (*ts'un*) ripple down over the hillsides — spontaneous imprints of the master's brush. Wang was particularly admired for his manner of rendering the "wrinkles" of mountains, the moss on the stones, the rugged pine-trees and the hidden depths of the gullies.

Spring in a mountain forest.
Wang Meng (d. 1385).

T'ao Ch'ien. Wang Chung Yu (14th century).
This portrait of T'ao Ch'ien executed in free-flow-
ing faint lines and inkwash (which are accentuated
by two darker lines in the form of a belt) attracts
by its extreme simplicity. Apparently there is no
background, only whiteness, but the figure stands
out nevertheless.

T'ao Ch'ien. Wong Chung Yu (14th C.).

165

In great contrast to Wang Chung Yu's *T'ao Yuan Ming* is the *Buddha under the Mango Tree* by Kwan Hsiu. The strokes are graceful and vibrant, like clouds and ripples on water. The straight staff lends variety to the flowing lines, giving them stability and support.

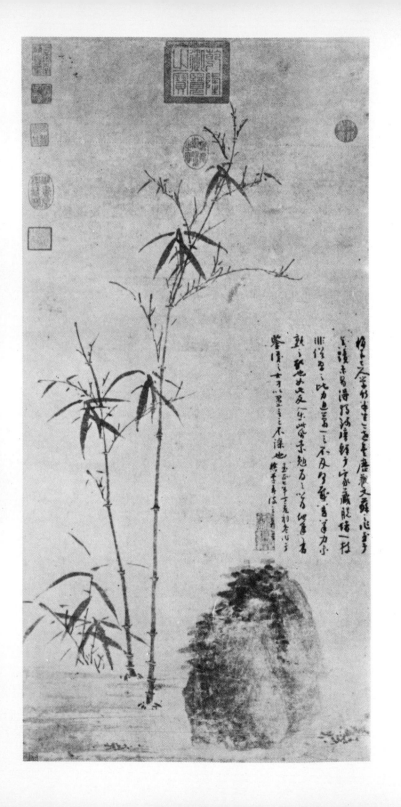

The painting on the opposite page is by Wu Chen (1280-1354) of the Yuan Dynasty. Wu drew inspiration from the great Wen Tung (see page 157), but here the leaves are more sparse than usual, distinguished however by consummate grace. The inscription says that he, the artist, has been learning to paint the bamboo for half of his life and that he is a great admirer of Wen Tung and Su Shih.

Returning Home by Donkey. T'ang Yin (1470-1524).
The inscription:

A failure, taking my books, I'm on my way home
Riding a mule again up the blue hills.
Tired of a world of wind, frost and dust,
I greet my wife, poor but not destitute.

A distinguishing feature of the painting is the way the rocky hills are structured. See how they twist and writhe — like watchful leopards with their backs toward the spectator — so powerfully picturesque, exciting and full of pathos.

Hsu Wei's versatility as painter, calligrapher, poet and dramatist entitles him to be called one of Ming Dynasty's great artists. In the picture opposite, the ink "colour" is extremely rich and full. The inscription forms part of the composition and balances the rock and banana trees.

The picture above is a section of a long hand scroll of flowers, fruit and trees, made up of irregular patches of inkwash, laid on spontaneously. "Movement" is the keyword to this cluster of vine and fruit which demonstrates brilliantly how an artist can manage ink to yield its many "colours."

Peonies. Ch'en Shun, 1483 - 1544.

Peonies. Ch'en Shun dated 1538
Ch'en was a brilliant flower painter. He developed
techniques in the use of ink to new heights of
coloristic beauty.

Landscape. Tung Chi Chang, 1555 - 1636. This was ▶
done in the manner of Mi Fu. It is interesting to
compare this with the ones by Lan Ying (P. 176)
and Yun Shuo Ping (P. 194).

174

Landscape. Lan Ying. 1585-1664.
The picture, as the inscription says, is done in the manner of Mi Fu, the Sung Dynasty painter and calligrapher who developed the "large dots" technique in the painting of hills, "Mi-dots" having

since become their name. Very few, if any, authentic Mi paintings have survived, and the picture above gives an excellent idea of what may possibly be the style of Mi.

Landscape. Mei Ching, 1623-1697.
Mei Ching's painting is done in the manner of Wu
Chen, but it holds its own as a model of elegance
and serenity. The dots are masterfully handled and
the texture is subtly applied. The inscription:

I love Wu Chen the plum-blossom sage,
Who works wondrous miracles with his brush.
He drinks the Immortals' wine of a thousand
	years;
And being wine-rapt, paints the South's eternal
	spring.

Rivers and Mountains without end (section of a hand-scroll). Hung-jen (c. 1603-1663).

This scene of autumn, with its austere lines and contours, reminds one of Ni Chan's landscapes. Alternation in the use of white and textured spaces is handled with great skill.

(Above) Queer looking bird. Pa Ta Shan Jen, 1625-c. 1705.
The significance of the "white eye" in the picture is this: the Chinese expression "giving someone the white eye" means "regarding someone with indifference and disdain." The artist was of royal descent. He refused to submit to the new Manchu regime, chose to be a recluse, and shunned all worldly contacts. Most of his paintings of birds and fish share that expression, as seen also in the picture opposite, the inscription on which is cryptic — quite unintelligible. This is intentional, as the artist did not want sympathizers of the new regime to know the real meaning; that would betray his real feeling.

Landscape. Shih T'ao (1641-c.1717).

It is a relief to look at this picture after seeing the usual fakes passed as authentic Shih-t'ao. There is a strange appeal in its splendid austerity — such economy of brushstrokes, every one of which vibrates with vitality. The variety of ink-tones is particularly interesting. The inscription reads:

When I left home in winter, the snow covered my hair.

Now I have seen two harvests in the barbarian
   land.
I am an outcast, but not thrown out like Su
   Shih;
A lonely person — who cares to indulge in wine?
Sadly I notice people here are tattooed and tall,
Though I do not mind living here for three
   autumns.
Having finally arrived in distant Weichou,
I only hope some news will reach me here.

Wild Ducks and Lotuses. Li Shan, Ching Dynasty.

The inscription:
In painting birds with ink and water,
Chao Meng-fu is well-known for his skill.
Underneath those wings what splendid colours lie,
Resting on the sand, beyond the reach of nets!
My host the premier has a fine collection of art
Exhilarating stuff to model on — I love doing it.
After staying a few days south of the city wall
I can now feel the soothing breeze of spring.

Landscape. Huang Shen, b. 1687.

Huang Shen was famous as a figure painter. This picture, however, has qualities which distinguish him as a supreme landscape artist. The beauty of his brushwork (seemingly so confused) is breathtaking, his individuality coming through with the strength of steel. Shades and dark spots are represented by lines. His brush strokes are so perfect that he need not resort to moss-dots for hiding flaws.

189

This fantasy by Kung Hsien is characterized by a
startling compactness. Clouds, waterfalls, cascades,
pools, trees and shrubs, and grotesque rocks all
spring to view as the eye runs through it. One is

fascinated by the seemingly haphazard positioning
of the solid rocks which nevertheless gives one a
feeling of inevitability.

Epidendra on rock side. Cheng Hsieh, 1693-
1765.
The inscription reads: My friend Yin Niu is strong
like the bamboo, pure like the epidendrum and
firm like rock. I know of none amongst my friends
who can claim to be his peer. He has asked me for
a painting several times, but I have not responded
so far. It is the fifth year of the realm of Chien
Lung, and he is on a visit. So I am giving him this
from amongst my own paintings. The bamboos are
without stems, the epidendrum leaves incline
towards one side and the rock leans outward. They
are hardly compatible with the ideals of the
virtuous man. To atone for this I shall do another
later on.

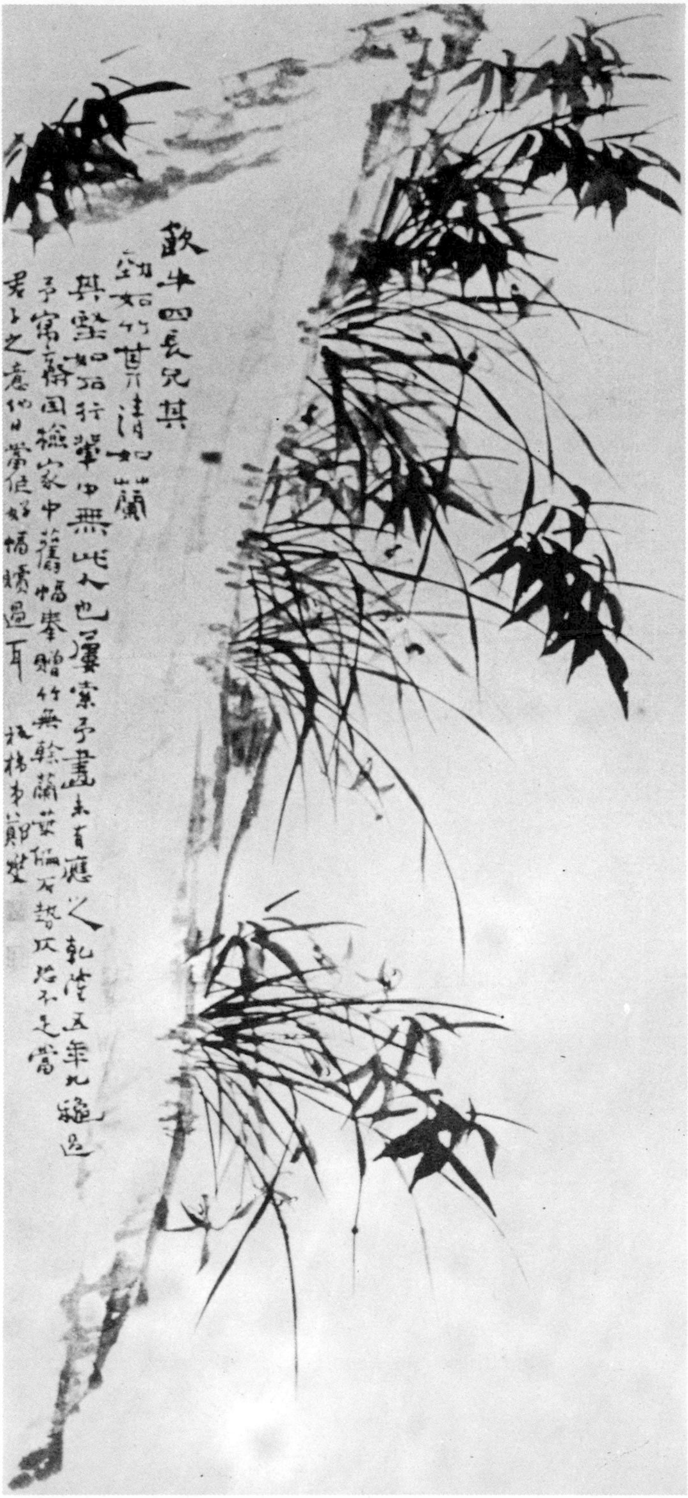

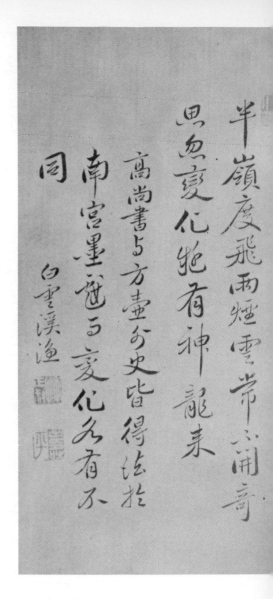

半嶺度飛雨煙雲常不開奇
與魚龍變化馳看神龍來
高尚書與方壺兮史皆得法於
南宮墨戲與變化不看不
同　白雲溪漁

Like the painting on P. 176-177, this is also
done in the manner of Mi Fu, by Yun Shou-ping.
The inscription, which includes a poem, reads:
    The rain glides quickly along the mountain
        range,
    Keeping within its domain the clouds and mists.

194

A strange thought has just come upon me:
A divine dragon has descended on earth.
Kao and Fang both take after Mi Fu in their ink-
play, but they have transformed it into something
quite different.

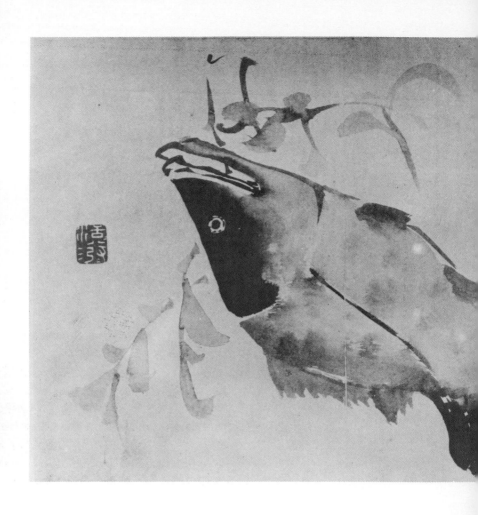

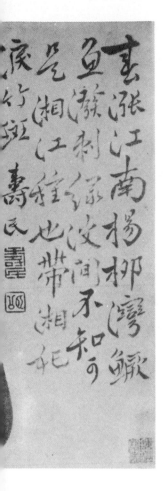

Perch. Pien Shuo-min, active 1725 - 1747.
The artist is well-known for his paintings of wild
ducks and fishes. One can almost feel the "wet-
ness" of the fish. The inscription reads: The willow
bay swells with the waters of spring, Perches frolic
in the green dancing waves. I wonder if they are
from the River Hsiang. Mark the tears of the wives
of Shun, that dapple this.*

* Tears of the Wives of Shun. Upon the death of Emperor
Shun (date of accession 2255 B. C.) his two wives wept so
much that their tears permanently dappled the bamboo on
which they dropped.

Landscape. Li K'uei, mid-19th century. A very
original composition that strikes one as taking after
masters such as Mei Ching and Shih T'ao. A temple
wall-decorator by profession, he achieved considerable eminence as a literary person. He was
most skillful in depicting the atmospheric and
transcendental qualities of the landscape.

Butterflies, bees, flowers and rock. Chu Lien, 1828-1904.

A charming arrangement by a specialist in flowers and insects. Chu was a leading member of the Lingnan School of Painting and wields great influence on the Kwangtung art scene.

He was particularly skilled at certain techniques including the application of water or white pigment to a damp area for special effect.

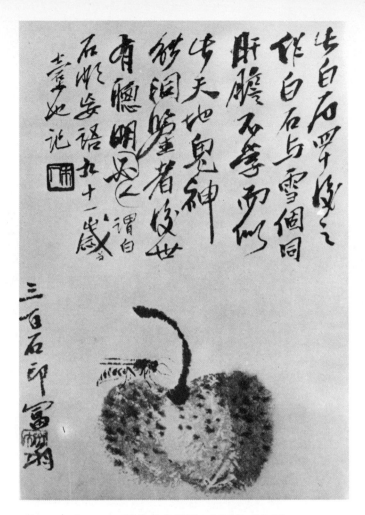

Pear and wasp. Ch'i Pai Shih, 1863–1957.
Ch'i Pai Shih is well-known for his child-like exuberance and his extraordinary skill in depicting subjects of everyday life, with a great economy of brushwork. He was an ardent admirer of Hsu Wei and Pa Ta Shan Jen. Here the inscription reads: This is a work of mine done after I was forty. My temperament and outlook are similar to Pa Ta's and my work is like his without my attempting to imitate him. The gods and Heaven know this well enough. Discerning people who come after me will agree that I am not just talking nonsense. Written at age ninety-one.

Landscape. Huang Pin Hung, 1864 - 1955.
This is a work of Huang's "middle" period — in his
sixties. The inscription says: In the use of brush
and ink, one should learn from the ancients and
adopt their methods. This can only be attained
through hard work and deep contemplation.

Detail.

This is a typical late work of Huang Pin Hung, 1864-1955. There is method in the mad disarray of brushstrokes which intrigue by their verve and vibrancy. The more one looks at it, the more one is fascinated by the bizarre composition. The inscription: The peaks of the Huang Mountains rise abruptly from the ground. When the sun's beams play with the fleeting clouds, their brilliance and splendour are indescribable. Painted at age 89.

(Note: Huang suffered temporary blindness probably soon after this painting was completed, but he continued painting throughout the period. He recovered from the blindness the following year.)

黄山諸峰拔地
而起四面清暁
日光雲影照
耀絢練不可言状
壬辰廬雖年少且九

By a lonesome pine. Pu Hsin Yu, 1896–1963.
This somber representation of a scholar is typical
of the traditional treatment of the subject. Pu was
an uncle of the deposed last Emperor of Imperial
China, and a scholar of eminence. His normal
mood is well described in the inscription:

I take my books and sit here without a care,
Dallying with a lonesome pine under its shade.
Perceiving how rapidly the clouds and every-
thing change,
I invite the evening sun to stay a little longer.
My pure hermit heart — What does it say?
Ten thousand chariots are but old shoes to me.

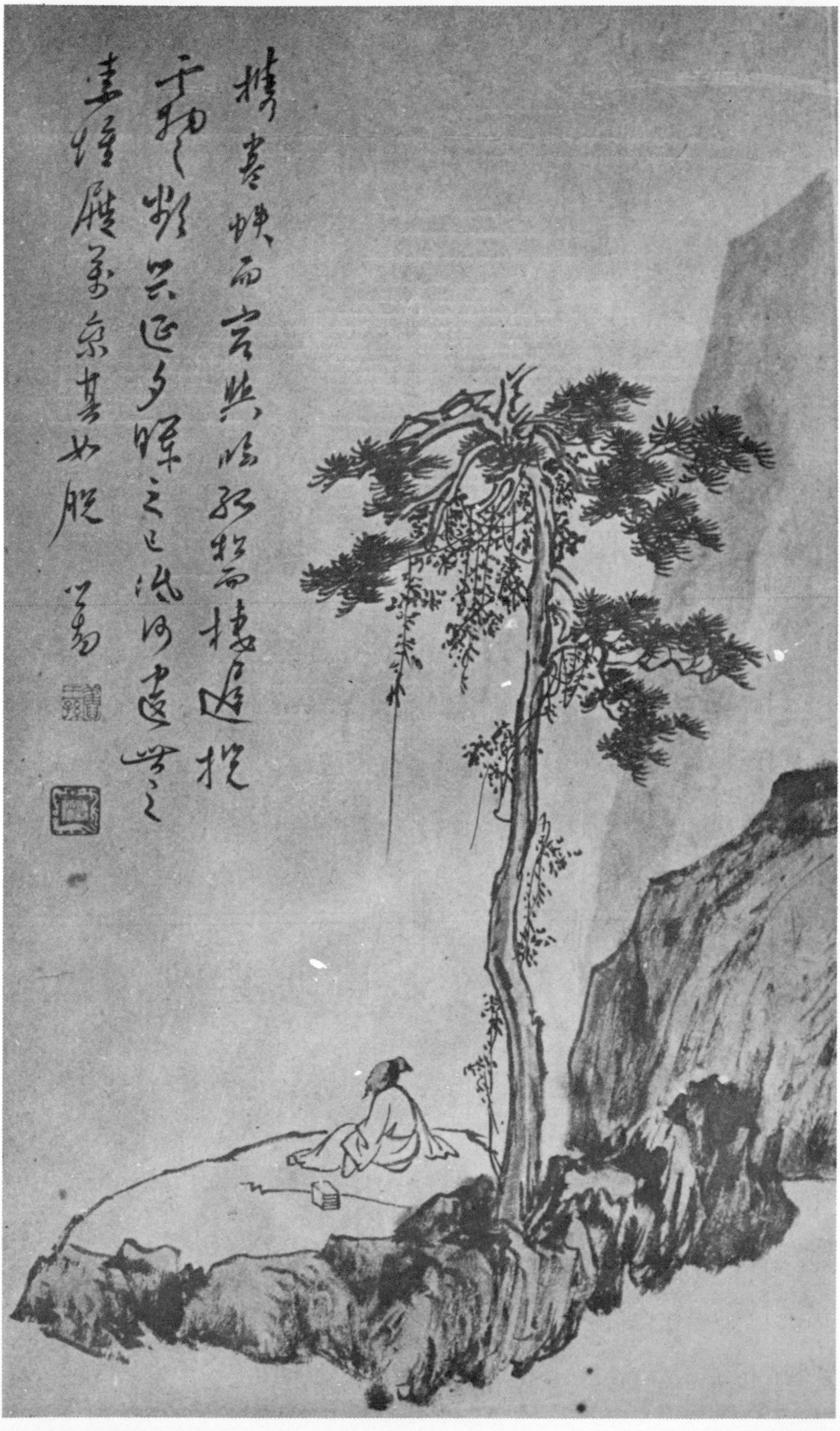

The Eight Immortals. Ting Yin-yung, 1905-1978.
Ting has a reputation for the skilful handling of the
brush. Here, every stroke can be accounted for.
"Spontaneous" can be the word used to describe
his way of "writing" the picture.
Old juniper. Lu Yen Shao, contemporary.   Little ▶
known outside China, this artist handles brush
and ink with consummate skill, as so powerfully
demonstrated here.

老檜
墨筆

Landscape. Jao Tsung I, contemporary. The simple, spontaneous calligraphic brush strokes speak for themselves — a fine demonstration of how a painting can be *written*.

Modern Chinese Painting:
Tradition and Innovations

by

Wucius Wong

Mr. Wucius Wong's essay represents one point of view in contemporary thinking on Chinese painting and its future, and is here presented as such.

It is written independently and without reference to the ideals and aesthetic preferences implicit in the contents of the book.

Modern Chinese Painting: Tradition and
Innovations

I

Chinese painting has never ceased developing.
There have always been two very different forces
which shape the path of Chinese painting: one is
the effort to maintain the tradition; another is the
search for individuality. These two forces, in appa-
rent conflict, often work together, with one at
times playing a more dominant role. Chinese painting has remained a separate, distinct category of
painting without being assimilated by Western art
in its worldwide significance.

Respect for tradition is a Confucian trait in the Chinese mentality. The Chinese people have always had a strong sense of history with an immense reverence for the past. At times of crisis, this could help to restore stability of society and re-establish national self-confidence and identity. Tradition being the accumulated wealth of the achievements of successive ages, it provides essential fertile ground for further growth though it seems to be a stumbling block to progress. The Chinese believe in the inheritance of the past for the blossoming of the future. It is in the past that the future takes root. This respect for tradition has probably made the Chinese people much less susceptible to foreign influences. It is not that the Chinese people are impervious to foreign influences; indeed foreign influences have always been integrated into Chinese civilization. The process of modernization in China necessarily takes a long time, for it must not be accomplished at the expense of tradition. Tradition has to be re-examined and re-evaluated from time to time, because certain weaknesses and shortcomings within the tradition could develop into a kind of cultural sickness which would undermine the original strength of the tradition.

The search for individuality, on the other hand, is accompanied by the need for the manifestation of the true self, a kind of thinking directly related to Taoism which contributed to the formation of the Chinese mentality almost as much as Confucianism. This force provides the very essence of artistic creativity. It conflicts with tradition only when the freedom of creativity is hampered. It generates the need for innovation and a breaking away from all conventions. Unlike the Westerners whose search for individuality tends to lay emphasis on the private sentiments of the personal ego, the Chinese seek a natural revelation of the natural state of the self, uncluttered by emotional fluctuations or conscious intellectuality.

Both Confucianism and Taoism put forward the concept of Tao which presupposes the perpetual existence of a harmonious order in Nature.Taoism, in particular, advocates the unveiling of the real personality toward the identification with Tao, and this leads to the communion with all things. Man and Nature, or spirit and matter, are one, a pervading theme which lies beneath the surface of most Chinese paintings.

The spirit of individuality is unique, free and independent, yet it conforms to the universal Tao. Thus the conflict between individuality and tradition does not necessarily exist, for Tao also incorporates tradition. What a creative Chinese artist seeks to do is to supercede all existing methods as imposed by tradition but not to deny or destroy the tradition. Individuality and tradition are complementary to each other like Yin and Yang, and the presence of both is essential for the uninterrupted continuity and vitality of Chinese culture.

II

It is certainly true that never before has tradition been so seriously challenged in China as in the last one hundred years. At the ultimate extreme, tradition was considered the main source of all evils in the society. The May 4th movement of 1919 to some extent highlighted this attitude, which remains influential still among some Chinese intellectuals of today. However, a total denial of tradition really means a total denial of everything that is intrinsically Chinese. How could this be possible, if one has to speak and think in the Chinese language most of the time, and live in an environment full of the Chinese past? There must be some kind of Chinese way of feeling and response toward things and events, inherited from one's parents.

A critical evaluation of tradition to form a basis for the reception of new ideas, concepts and technology from the West is practically the only way to modernization. In an age of transition, the general situation is that there is stubborn conservatism on one side, and blind rebellion against tradition on the other, resulting in conflict and confusion of aims and standards. The art scene of twentieth-century China is very much a microcosm of this cultural turmoil. There are artists, usually of the older generation, who continue to practise traditional Chinese painting with little concern for the changing spirit of the time. They repeat the styles of masters of the past and work on the same kind of subject matter and composition with the same kind of tools, materials and techniques. Reacting against this sort of traditionalism are those probably younger in age, who choose to follow Western trends. Some do espouse realism in the style of the nineteenth century, while others are more attracted to the exploratory spirit of Western art of today.

It may be necessary to point out that Western ideas of art education have now been commonly adopted in the educational systems from which the new generations emerge. Western realism enables one to draw or paint what they see before them and this skill is usually lacking among the traditionalists. Modern Western art ranging from Fauvism and Cubism to abstract and conceptual art and beyond encourages individual experimentation. Painters using Western media such as oil or acrylic pigments are generally called Western style painters regardless of their styles being abstract or realistic. The traditionalists are simply called "traditional Chinese painters."

Creative artists are no followers of any trend, for they anticipate and try to lead the trends. One could say that the traditionalists are generally conservative, whereas the Western style painters have a more liberal attitude toward innovation. It is surprising, however, that no artists of any great significance have so far emerged among the latter, except a few who have settled down in the West and achieved considerable fame in the contemporary art scene there. On the contrary, quite a number of prominent traditionalists attained high individual accomplishment in the first half of the twentieth century. They were able to go beyond the confines of the mummified tradition in their final years, after a persistent pursuit of a lifetime.

The main motivating force in modern Chinese painting, especially after the mid-century, is from those who do not distinctly belong to any of the two categories of artists mentioned above. In a sense they are neither completely loyal to tradition nor totally drawn to styles and trends of Western art. Some have started with a background in traditional Chinese painting but have looked West for innovative ideas. Others with a solid foundation in Western art have found their way back to the tradition but with a totally new vision.

III

If modern Chinese art is to have a significant place in the art world, it must not merely give what the world already has, but strive to supply something original. Originality is to be sought within the heart of each individual artist and the root of artistic growth lies in one's cultural heritage. Therefore it is natural that in the middle of a Chinese artist's career, he would instinctively embrace tradition in order to find his true self. There are instances of Chinese artists who would, after spending some time abroad in pursuit of painting in a Western trend and having returned to China, take up the Chinese brush and ink and rice paper for their artistic expression. Many switched to more traditional Chinese painting after practising Western-style painting for a number of years.

In all such cases, the artist is like the prodigal son who gradually finds his way home. Whether these artists move back very close to tradition or still try to experiment, the first things they reach for are the traditional tools and materials. Significantly when a traditionalist wants to do something more relevant to the contemporary world, it is extremely unlikely that he throws his Chinese brush and ink away. How important is the medium itself in artistic expression? Why do many Chinese artists still use the traditional medium?

Chinese ink has the capacity of providing an unsurpassed range of tones ranging from the clearest shades to the densest blacks. All marks made on absorbent rice paper are permanent and irremovable, for they do not remain on the surface but are soaked into the fibres of the paper. Water and ink and most Chinese colours are transparent, and there is nothing on the surface of the paper which can be physically felt. The images expressed in this way have a tendency to recede very much behind the picture plane.

The Chinese brush is soft and springy and it readily transmits all forces and vibrations of the hand which holds it. Its hair comes to a point easily, and where this point lies on the path of a drawn line with the brush is important in determining the character of the line. Lines and dots can build textures for the description of forms, and each line or dot is more or less a kind of personal calligraphy of the artist. Un-inked areas are as important as the inked areas. It must be pointed out also that there is no tactile difference between the inked and the un-inked areas on a Chinese painting.

By comparison, oil paint is viscuous and largely opaque when applied thickly. The substance of the medium is deposited on the surface of a piece of canvas and forms a new surface which hides what is underneath, and it is a rare practice to expose any part of the bare canvas which has a different texture from what is made by the paint. The range of colours is extremely wide and full brilliance can be even further enhanced by adding on a coat of glossy varnish. Brush strokes can be rough and lumpy, but they can also be unrecognizable with very smooth application of paint. Correction is generally possible. Colour modelling is more suited to this kind of medium than linear expression.

Choice for the medium considerably determines the kind of work produced. The directness, transparency, fluidity and immateriality of the Chinese ink medium indeed appeal more to the Chinese nature in seeking communion with Tao than the oil medium which has much more of a material presence. The qualities inherent in the medium remain unchanged in spite of the changes in visual elements on the painting. Thus the insistence on the medium of water and Chinese ink on absorbent paper by many modern Chinese artists establishes an essential link with the tradition and a point of departure for individual innovations. Innovations can be made in many directions. Each artist relates himself to tradition in different distances and angles, and the distances and angles could change during the various stages of his creative career. A new tradition is in the making and every serious effort to innovate contributes to this.

One obvious direction of innovation is in the widening of the choice of subject matter as present in traditional Chinese painting. Machinery, modern construction works, and many other things in our contemporary environment are not considered as unsuitable for a Chinese painting. The composition and general pictorial presentation may be affected by the introduction of these elements. Many such paintings executed in the traditional manner naturally reflect the influence of Western realism, with the integration of scientific perspective, light and shade modelling, and anatomical structure in figures and animals.

Another direction is in the exploration of new visual possibilities with the traditional medium. The Chinese brush, ink and paper are all used in unusual ways for unexpected effects, sometimes with the combination of new tools and materials. Some artists go as far as rejecting the traditional completely and seek controllable accidental effects by dyeing, staining, rubbing, printing, spraying, and whatever techniques they can think of. Such experimentations often lead to more abstract work, but landscapes of traditional mood are sometimes suggested in the textural compositions.

Abstraction is a quality that is more associated with Chinese art than Western art, although painting in total abstraction is first reached by Western artists in the twentieth century. The Chinese artist, however, has for centuries nourished a supreme art form of calligraphy and often regards the expression of the spirit far more important than the mere portrayal of the external appearance of things. Those who live and work outside mainland China with the awareness of what is currently happening in contemporary Western art are interested in new concepts and ideas which can be expressed in traditional Chinese ink. Many of such experiments are probably still immature and perhaps attempted in isolation, but the vitality is there, and the diversified pursuits have at least demonstrated that the traditional Chinese ink medium has its unique characteristics which cannot be replaced by any Western painting medium. And if the medium continues to be favoured by most Chinese artists of today, it is justifiable to say that the Chinese painting tradition is not dead, but is undergoing a new phase of development.

When one looks back from the 21st century, the present will not be seen as a great century of artistic activity for China — that could only spring from a long period of stability and prosperity. The country has seen revolutions and wars and changes occuring at such a rapid pace, widening the gap between older and younger generations, and between people of different social strata and educational backgrounds. Artists who strive to establish personal visions which demand new standards of aesthetic judgment run the risk of not being immediately understood and accepted. Thus it is likely for the pioneers to suffer failure to find proper recognition during their lifetime, and proper recognition is likely to be denied to the pioneers until their influence begins to be felt at a later date.

Huang Pin-hung: Landscape.　　　　　　　▶
A highly individual style emerges after almost a life-long pursuit of the tradition. Dense brush strokes spread in multi-layers across the picture plane with strong rhythmical quality.

◄ Ch'i Pai-shih: Shrimps
A new subject matter is expressed in a
naturalistic manner, exploring a wide
range of transparent ink tones. The
play of entwined lines in contrast with
the wet ink spots could be viewed as
an abstract composition.

Hsu Pei-hung: Willows and Birds   ►
Western realism and Chinese brush-work
are fused together in this powerful work.
Note in the portrayal of the birds, the use
of foreshortening which is extremely rare
in Chinese painting.

Fu Pao-shih: A Winter Scene
The hair of the Chinese brush is intentionally disarranged for
unusual textural effects. Resulting mountain forms tend to be
rather indefinite, bordering on abstraction.

224   Kao Chien-fu: Sepia
       The painting features dominantly ink washes in tonal gradation
       and is nearly formless except for the petal-like arms of the
       sepia enveloped in their dark secretions.

Lin Feng-mien: Seated Lady
Simple flowing lines mark the graceful contour of the figure. Opaque colours are
applied on paper in thick patches resembling oil painting techniques.

Li K'o Jan: Scenery at Yang Sho
Strong light-and-shade modelling enhances solidity and depth. This is a painting
from direct observation expressed in traditional brushwork.

Cheng Shih-fa: Shepherdess
Bold calligraphic strokes are matched by thin, twisted, deft
lines, revealing interesting figurative elements in a rather
abstract composition.

Lui Shou Kwan: Abstract
Sweeping strokes and splashed ink create a world of total
abstraction. The feeling of a landscape theme, with mountains,
trees and the horizon, is still quite strong.

Appendixes

Essentials of painting

Spirit (*ch'i*) is obtained when your mind moves along with the movement of the brush and does not hesitate in delineating images.

Resonance (*yün*) is obtained when you establish forms while hiding traces of the brush, and perfect them by observing the proprieties and avoiding vulgarity.

Thought (*ssu*) is obtained when you grasp essential forms eliminating unnecessary details in your observation of nature, and let your ideas crystallize into the forms to be represented.

Scene (*cheng*) is obtained when you study the laws of nature and the different faces of time, look for the sublime, and recreate it with reality.

Brush (*pi*) is obtained when you handle the brush freely, applying all the varieties of strokes in accordance with your purpose, although you must follow certain basic rules of brushwork. Here you should regard brushwork neither as substance nor as form but rather as a movement, like flying or driving. Ink (*mo*) is obtained when you distinguish higher and lower parts of objects with a gradation of ink tones and represent clearly shallowness and depth, thus making them appear as natural as if they had not been done with a brush.

Four types of "force" in brushwork: *muscle, flesh, bone* and *spirit*. If a stroke is discontinued but its force continues, its force is called *muscle*. If a stroke with thickening and thinning width is filled with substantial inner force, its force is called *flesh*. If a stroke is vigorous and upright, with force to give life to dead matter, it is called *bone*. If each stroke delineating the whole painting is undefeatable, the total force is called *spirit*.

from Ching Hao's, Pi Fa-Chi

Transl. K. Munakata

Appendix II

Six Prerequisites of Excellence in Painting as prescribed by

Hsieh Ho (A.D. 479—501) in *Ku Hua Pin Lu*

(1) Rhythmic Vitality

The artist should strive to perceive the spirit of the subject and recreate it with a powerful brush and beautiful ink tones.

(2) Significant brushwork

Skilled manipulation of the brush, which is an extension of the artistic mind, is developed by prolonged practice and leads to deft and significant brushwork.

(3) Likeness according to nature

Portraying the spirit through the form requires the ability to draw good likenesses.

(4) Appropriate ink-tones or colouring

The colours of a painting should match the hues of nature.

(5) Creative composition

To achieve a sense of three-dimensional space, careful planning is required.

(6) Creative modelling

In the process of modelling upon ancient great art, the artist should impart a creative touch of his own.

Some Quotations

To judge a painting by its verisimilitude betrays the intellectual level of a child. (Su Shih, 1036-1101 A.D.)

Mountain and rivers have a material form and yet intrigue the spirit (Tsung Ping: *Preface to Landscape Painting* 375-443 A.D.)

Formal likeness and basic individuality come from the artist's conception of the subject and are based ultimately upon brushwork. That is why a good painter is usually a good calligraphist. (Chang Yen-yüan: *Li-tai Ming-hua Chi*, dated 847)

Drawing bows and knives and columns and beams could be done without a ruler or guiding line by full concentration of the mind. Drawings done with a ruler look dead. (Summarised from a paragraph in *Li-tai Ming-hua Chi* by Chang Yen-yüan.)

There are four moving qualities of the brush-lines: tendons, flesh, bones, and strength or vigour. Where the lines break off and yet remain connected in line space — that is the tendons. Where the movements, beginning and end, are full and well formed — that is the flesh. Where the lifeline is strong and straight — that is the bones. Where there are no weak lines — that is the strength of spirit. Therefore it is seen that overuse of ink spoils the form; pale, insufficient shading spoils the vigour; dead tendons spoil the flesh; completely disjointed lines are lacking in tendons; and the merely pretty lack bones. (Ching Hao fl. 920 A.D.)

(This is a variation of the passage entitled Four Types of Force in Brushwork on page 233.)

Poem written on the wall of a friend's house:
"Receiving the moisture of wine
My intestines sprout and fork out,
And from out my liver and lungs
Shoot rocks and bamboos,
Surging through my breast, irresistible,
They find expression on your snow-white wall."
                    (Su Shih. Transl. Lin Yutang)

When one is not equal to painting, the best thing is to take a stroll alone. Perhaps one will encounter nothing, or perhaps one will come across an odd piece of rock, or a dried-up branch, a small pool, or a sparse wood. These things lie about, unwanted by anybody. But they are pieces of nature, totally unlike what is seen in pictures. One should give them a cool, careful look and try to catch that indefinable quality wherein lies the expression of life. This is like poets jotting down lines to be incorporated in verses later.

Students of art fall into ruts as soon as they begin. But women and children and unpretentious people often draw for their own pleasure, and are afraid to show their paintings to others. Such drawings may not be lifelike, but they have something which the accomplished artists do not have — freshness and naivete. (Ku Ning-yüan fl. 1570)

There are seven types of calamities that can happen to painting and calligraphy: (1) When prices are too high, they are above the reach of the common people. As a result, the works of art all go into collections of the wealthy, where genuine works are lumped together with the spurious. (2) When a noble family falls and its property is confiscated, the collections all go to the imperial court where they are eaten by moths and insects and can no longer be seen by the people. (3) Vulgar people collect art objects for reputation and professional dealers compete in raising the prices, without regard to their intrinsic worth. (4) Great, powerful dealers trade them like goods and are willing to part with them for a profit. Then the works go into the possession of the vulgarians. (5) The works are locked in rich mansions, their cases covered with dust, while the owners gorge themselves with food. (6) Uneducated heirs of fortune do not care a bit about these family possessions and seem totally unconcerned in case of fire or theft. (7) The works are sometimes spoiled through bad, unskilled mountings, and facial features are destroyed, or substitutes are made, causing disputes.

I am as I am; I exist. I cannot stick the whiskers of the ancients on my face, nor put their entrails in my belly. I have my own entrails and chest, and I prefer to twitch my own whiskers. If sometimes by chance I happen to resemble someone, it is he who happens to come to me, and not I who try to be his death. This is the way it is. Why should I model myself upon the ancients and not develop my own forte?

On Brush and Ink. Among the ancients, some have brush (-technique) but no ink (-technique). Others have ink (-technique) but no brush (-technique). The difference lies in the man's natural talent.

(Shin T'ao 1641 – 1717. trans. Lin Yutang)

When the brush contacts paper, there are only differences in touch, speed, angle and direction. But a too light touch results in weakness while a too heavy touch causes clumsiness. Too much speed results in a slippery effect, too little speed drags; too much slant (of brush tip) results in thinness; a curve may have ragged edges and a straight line may look like one made with a ruler. All these come from lack of flexibility and too much effort. Things and objects vary infinitely in form and manner, and it is possible to capture them all by the brush stroke.

Artists who do not understand the secret of brush work and ink work often go for striking effects by using bizarre forms. That is why modern art is sinking daily into vulgarity.

Chao Meng-fu says, "A child hardly weaned starts to paint in the morning and in the evening boasts of his skill." Really such a person still smells of his mother's milk. It takes ten years for an artist to gain familiarity with painting materials, another ten years to complete the general training and yet another ten to be able to develop his own style.

The good student is too busily concerned with corrections of his shortcomings to be thinking of sudden popularity. The reward will come to him inevitably with maturity of his craft. Therefore I say, "Avoid early popularity in order to reach a higher goal."

(Shen Tsung Chien, fl. 1781)

GLOSSARY

Chang Feng	張風		Li Shan	李山
Chang Ku	張谷		Li Shan	李鱓
Chang Ting	張汀		Li Tsai	李在
Chang Yen-yuan	張彥遠		Li Yu	李漁
Chao Meng-chien	趙孟堅		Lin Feng-mien	林風眠
Chen Hung-shuo	陳洪綬		Lo Pin	羅聘
Ch'en Shun	陳淳		Lu Yen Shao	陸儼少
Cheng Hsieh	鄭燮		Lui Shou Kwan	呂壽琨
Ch'eng Shih Fa	程十髮		Mei Ching	梅清
Ch'i Pai Shih	齊白石		Mu Chi	牧溪
Chieh Tzu Yüan	芥子園畫傳		Ni Tsan	倪瓚
Hua Chuan			Pa Ta Shan Jen	八大山人
Chin Nung	金農		*Pi Fa Chi*	筆法記
Ching Hao	荊浩		Pien Shuo-min	邊壽民
Ch'iu Ying	仇英		Pu Hsin-yü	溥心畬
Fan Kan	范寬		Shen Chou	沈周
Fu Chi	符翕		Shen Tsung Chien	沈宗騫
Fu Pao-shih	傅抱石		Shih Lo	石洛
Fu Shan	傅山		Shih T'ao	石濤
Hsieh Ho	謝赫		Su Jen Shan	蘇仁山
Hsu Pei-hung	徐悲鴻		Su Shih	蘇軾
Hsu Wei	徐渭		T'ang Yin	唐寅
Huang Chuan	黃荃		Ting Yin-yung	丁衍鏞
Huang Pin Hung	黃賓虹		Tu Fu	杜甫
Huang Shen	黃慎		Tung Chi Chang	董其昌
Huang T'ing Chien	黃庭堅		Tung Yüan	董源
Hui Tsung	徽宗		Wang Hsi-chih	王羲之
Hung Jen	弘仁		Wang Hsien Chih	王獻之
Ko Chiu Sze	柯九思		Wang Mien	王冕
Ku An	顧安		Wang Wei	王維
Ku Kai Chih	顧愷之		Wang Yuan-chi	王原祈
Kung Hsien	龔賢		Wen Tung	文同
Kuo Hsi	郭熙		Wu Chang Shih	吳昌碩
Kwan Hsiu	貫休		Wu Chen	吳鎮
Lan Ying	藍瑛		Wu Kung Tsai	伍公采
Li Cheng	李成		Yun Shuo Ping	惲壽平
Li Ko Jan	李可染			